Extreme Sports

Rock Climbing

by Bill Lund

CAPSTONE PRESS
MANKATO, MINNESOTA

C A P S T O N E   P R E S S
818 North Willow Street • Mankato, MN 56001

Printed in the United States of America.

Library of Congress Cataloging-in-Publication Data
Lund, Bill, 1954-
    Rock Climbing/by Bill Lund
    p. cm. -- (extreme sports)
    Includes bibliographical references and index.
    Summary: Describes the history, equipment, and contemporary practice of rock climbing.
    ISBN 1-56065-429-5
    1. Rock climbing--Juvenile literature. [1. Rock climbing] I. Title.
II. Series.
GV200.2.L86 1996
796.552'3--dc20

                                96-24724
                                   CIP
                                   AC

Photo credits
International Stock/Mark Newman, 10. Greg Vaughn, 22. W. Lynn Seldon Jr., 30. Joe Staudenbaur, cover, 34, 38. Unicorn, 6, 12; David P. Dill, 8; Tommy Dodson, 24, 36; Rod Furgason, 17; Jean Higgins, 14, 41; Ron Holt, 4; Marie Mills, 32; Marshall R. Prescott, 26; Larry Stanley, 20; Lee Watson, 19; Dick Young, 42; Gary L. Johnson, 28.

Table of Contents

Words in **boldface** type in the text are defined
in the Glossary in the back of this book.

Chapter 1

Climbing to the Top

Many people think of exotic peaks when they think of rock climbing. Some imagine Alaska's snow-capped Mount McKinley. Others imagine Mount Everest, the tallest mountain in the world.

But most rock climbing is done on smaller hills and cliffs. Rock-climbing **terrain** can be found in almost every state and province in North America. Different terrain appeals to different kinds of climbers.

Almost any hill, valley, mountain, or cliff is interesting to rock climbers. All a rock climber needs is a **rock face**. Then they can boost

Many people think of such exotic peaks as Mount McKinley when they think of rock climbing.

themselves up with their feet. They can balance with their hands.

Rock Climbers

Rock climbers are amateur athletes. Rock climbers do not have to be big, tall, or strong. Most rock climbers enjoy the beauty of the natural world. They like difficult physical activity, too.

Rock climbers enjoy seeing new places. They give themselves new challenges. They want to explore places high above their heads.

Rock climbers can be any age. There are rock climbers who are not yet teenagers. Some people climb rocks until they are 90 years old or older.

Mountain Climbing

Some climbers advance from hills to mountains. Mountains are the world's highest rock formations. Mountains usually have many

Rock climbers enjoy seeing new places.

cliffs and rock faces. Just one of them could be as difficult to climb as a single hill.

The difference between a mountain and a hill is the height. The peak of a mountain is usually at least 1,000 feet (300 meters) above **sea level**. There is no set height, though, that says exactly when a hill becomes a mountain. It is different from country to country.

Dangers

Rock climbing can be a lot of fun. But it can be dangerous, too. There is always the chance that a climber will fall.

The best climbers are aware of the dangers. They make sure they have good equipment. They make sure they do not try to climb a rock face they are not experienced enough to climb. They make sure their clothing is suited to the weather.

Many things can go wrong when a climber is on a rock face. Good climbers do everything they can to make sure things go right. Good climbers live to climb again and again.

The best climbers have good equipment.

Chapter 2
History

People have not always been interested in rock climbing. Many ancient people thought powerful spirits lived on mountain peaks. They believed it was wise to avoid mountains.

The ancient Greeks believed in many different gods. They thought these gods lived at the top of a mountain called Olympus. People who climbed mountains might make the gods angry.

These ancient beliefs eventually died out. People became curious about mountains and hills. Some climbed mountains just to see what

Many ancient people thought powerful spirits lived on mountains.

was on the other side. Many others climbed rocks for practical reasons.

People could see long distances from the tops of hills. They could see what their neighbors were doing. If they were at war, they could spy on their enemies.

Sometimes people climbed mountains to get minerals. People have climbed mountains looking for gold. Others were looking for food. Some climbers hunted mountain animals.

Climbing As a Sport

Rock climbing as a sport officially began in 1760. That was the year prize money was offered to the first person who climbed Mont Blanc. The prize was offered by a scientist from Switzerland.

Mont Blanc is a mountain located between France and Italy. Mont Blanc is 15,771 feet (4,731 meters) tall. It is the highest mountain in Europe.

Mont Blanc is in Switzerland, between France and Italy.

Mont Blanc is difficult to climb. The prize money was not claimed until 1786. That was when Dr. Michel Paccard and Jacques Balmat climbed to the top. They were both from Switzerland.

Many Europeans started climbing mountains as a sport in the 1800s. They climbed mountains in a range called the Alps. The Alps are mostly in Austria, Germany, Switzerland, Italy, and France. Mont Blanc is in the Alps.

The Matterhorn

The most famous early climb took place on a peak called the Matterhorn in Switzerland. The Matterhorn is 14,692 feet (4,408 meters) tall. It is the third tallest mountain in the Alps.

The Matterhorn has very steep sides. It is shaped like a pyramid. Its peak is almost always covered with snow.

The Matterhorn is very difficult to climb. Many climbers had tried. None had ever made it to the top.

Edward Whymper was an English explorer. He led a group of seven English climbers up

The Matterhorn has steep sides.

15

the Matterhorn in 1865. They reached the top on July 14.

On the way down, four of the climbers fell and died. They fell nearly a mile (about 1.5 kilometers). Some people said the climbers who fell were inexperienced. Some people believed spirits knocked the climbers off the mountain. More people have died trying to climb the Matterhorn than any other mountain in the Alps.

English explorers climbed every major mountain in Europe. Over the next 30 years, English explorers climbed nearly every major mountain on the continents of North America, South America, and Africa.

The Himalayas

In the early 1900s, mountain climbers looked for other challenges. They turned their attention to the Himalayan mountains. They had climbed everything else.

Mountain climbers always look for new challenges.

The Himalayas are in southern Asia. They are in the countries of Nepal, Tibet, and India. The world's 14 tallest mountains are there.

K2 is in the Himalayas. K2 is 28,250 feet (8,611 meters) above sea level. It is the second highest mountain in the world. In 1902, a British team tried to climb K2. They were not successful.

Mount Everest is in the Himalayas. Mount Everest is the world's tallest mountain. The top of Mount Everest is more than 29,028 feet (8,708 meters) above sea level. In 1922 and 1924, British teams tried to climb Mount Everest. They were not successful.

Annapurna is in the Himalayas. Annapurna is 26,504 feet (8,078 meters) above sea level. A French team climbed Annapurna in 1950.

The Top of Mount Everest

A group of more than 400 climbers, guides, and helpers tried to climb Mount Everest in 1953. This group had an advantage that early

Climbers are not always successful.

climbers did not have. Their equipment was lightweight.

Early mountain climbers had heavy equipment. Their clothes were thick. Their boots had iron spikes in the soles.

The equipment got better as the sport got older. New materials were used to make lighter clothes and equipment. The 1953 group carried oxygen tanks, too.

The air high in the mountains has less oxygen in it than air closer to sea level. Most people are not used to the thin mountain air. The oxygen in the tanks helped the climbers work harder and rest better.

Two people from the group made it to the top of Mount Everest on May 29, 1953. They were Edmund Hillary, a New Zealander, and Tenzing Norgay, a **Sherpa** tribe member. They were the first people in the world to stand on top of the world's highest mountain.

Air high in the mountains is hard to breathe.

People travel to Washington state to climb Mount Rainier.

The Mountains of North America

The highest mountain in North America is Mount McKinley. Mount McKinley is in Alaska. It is 20,320 feet (6,096 meters) tall.

A man from the United States climbed to the top of Mount McKinley in 1913. The man's name was Hudson Stuck.

Canada's highest mountain is Mount Logan. Mount Logan is in the Yukon. It is 19,850 feet (5,955 meters) tall. Mount Logan is only a little shorter than Mount McKinley. A team of climbers from Canada and the United States reached the top of Mount Logan in 1925.

Climbing Smarter

The first climbs up the highest mountains were huge expeditions. There were hundreds of people in some of the climbing groups. Today, the trend is to climb these mountains in smaller groups.

In 1975, two Austrians climbed a mountain called Hidden Peak. Hidden Peak is in the Himalayas. It is 26,470 feet (7,941 meters) tall.

The climbers were Reinhold Messner and Peter Habeler. Nobody thought that two people would make it to the top alone. People had climbed the highest moutains only in large groups.

Twelve people helped carry Messner and Habeler's equipment to the base of the mountain. The 12 helpers did not climb, though. Messner and Habeler made it to the top by themselves in three days.

There were more climbing advances in the late 1970s. Messner and others climbed some of the highest mountains without oxygen tanks. Nobody thought it could be done until Messner and others did it.

Chapter 3
Climbing Techniques

Rock climbing can be very enjoyable. But it can also be dangerous. Climbers must know what they are doing.

Even experienced climbers can fall and injure themselves. Rock climbers should be well trained before they take on their first cliffs. Part of the challenge of rock climbing is being prepared.

Finding Holds

Rock climbers must find spots where they can fit a hand or a foot. These spots for hands

Climbers find places to fit their hands and feet.

Climbers try to position their bodies directly above their feet.

and feet are called holds. Holds allow climbers to pull or push themselves up.

A hold must be two things. It must be big enough for the climber's foot or hand to fit into it. It must also be secure enough to hold the climber's weight.

Rock climbers look for any kind of knob, **outcropping**, or ledge. A large hold is called a bucket. A very small hold is called a finger because a finger is all that will fit there.

Sometimes climbers cannot find any holds. Then they look for a long vertical crack. If they find one, they force part of their body into the opening. This is called jamming. Climbers can work their way up the cliff by jamming their bodies higher and higher in the crack.

Balance is important in rock climbing. Climbers try to position their body weight directly above their feet. Climbers can see and reach footholds and handholds best when they are in a balanced position.

Smart Climbing

Smart climbers look ahead. They study the rock above them. They plan what their next moves will be.

Smart climbers move only one leg or one arm at a time. This helps them stay balanced. If they are balanced, they are less likely to fall.

Smart climbers test holds before they use them. They wiggle each new hold with their hand or foot. They put their weight on a hold slowly. They test holds to make sure they are secure.

Rappelling

Once rock climbers get to the top of a hill or mountain, they need a way to get down. Many climbers learn how to **rappel**. Rappelling is a special way to go down a hill or mountain.

When climbers rappel, they anchor a rope at the top of a cliff. They hold the rope in a special way around their waist. Often, they use a harness. Rappellers move down the cliff by sliding down the rope.

Rappelling is an exciting way to go down a rock face. Rappelling is good for steep cliffs where any other way down might be too dangerous. If they can drive or walk to the top, some rappellers do not climb at all. They like

Rappelling is a special way to go down a rock face.

going down a cliff more than they like going up one.

Artificial Rock Faces

When most people think of rock climbing, they think of the great outdoors. But rock climbing does not have to be done outdoors. Some climbers tackle artificial rock faces that are indoors.

Some of these artificial rock faces are made of wood. Others are made of stone and concrete. Some of them are huge fireplaces.

Artificial rock faces have good handholds and footholds. Many have padding on the ground in case the climbers fall. Artificial rock faces can be found in sports centers, sporting goods stores, or even shopping malls.

Artificial rock faces are good for beginners. Inexperienced climbers can train without worrying about getting hurt if they fall. They can decide if rock climbing is a sport they want to take up.

Some people climb artificial rock faces.

Chapter 4
Safe Climbing

Safe climbers make sure they have the right equipment. They know that good equipment will reduce the chances of a fall. Good equipment can be the difference between life and death.

The best climbers keep safety in mind. They are well trained. They concentrate on what they are doing at all times.

Many people think that rock climbers need strong arms. This is a myth, though. Most climbing is done with the legs. A climber's arms are used mostly for balance.

Safe climbers have the right equipment.

Rock climbers do need to be physically fit, though. They also need to be **limber**. Rock climbers must be able to concentrate hard. Concentration helps them find the best path up a rock face.

Scrambling

Scrambling is one type of climbing. Scrambling requires no special equipment. Scramblers use only their hands and feet.

Scrambling can be done only when the top is not too high and the rock face is not too dangerous. Scramblers use handholds and footholds to move up easy-to-climb hills and cliffs. Anyone from a hiker to a serious climber can be a scrambler.

High and Difficult Climbs

Many experienced rock climbers like higher and more difficult climbs.

If they are lucky, there is a road or path to the top of the rock face they want to climb. At the top, they look for a sturdy rock or tree. They can use the rock or tree as an anchor.

Scramblers use only their hands and feet to climb.

Climber

Hand Hold

Foot Hold

Climbers use clips called carabiners.

Climbers attach **webbing** to any anchors
they find. Webbing is made of very strong
nylon strips. Climbers attach a carabiner to the
webbing. A carabiner is a heavy aluminum
clip. It connects the webbing to a kernmantle
rope.

Kernmantle ropes are made of nylon. The nylon is covered with a woven material. Kernmantle ropes are strong and flexible. They will hold up climbers who fall. Because they are flexible, they do not jerk climbers too hard.

When the equipment is set up, the two ends of the kernmantle rope hang down from the anchor. They hang all the way to the bottom of the cliff. This type of climb requires two people. One person is the climber. One end of the rope is tied to the climber.

The other end of the rope is tied to the **belayer**. The belayer stays at the bottom of the rock face. The belayer watches the rope. The belayer keeps the rope tight at all times.

The belayer's job is to stop the climber if he or she falls. As long as the rope is tight, the belayer can keep the climber from falling far.

The Piton

Often, there is no path or road leading to the top of a rock face. Then climbers have no way to set up an anchor. They use a piton. A piton is a metal spike with a ring on one end.

The lead climber pounds the piton into the rock. He or she pulls the kernmantle rope through the ring in the piton. The piton is used as an anchor.

The lead climber goes up the mountain. He or she puts in more pitons as they are needed. The lead climber's pitons can be used as anchors for other climbers.

Clean Climbing

Many rock climbers have been conscious of the environment since the early 1970s. They have made changes in their equipment. The new equipment does less damage to the rocks.

Climbers in North America found that steel pitons were damaging the rocks. They invented aluminum chocks. Aluminum is a soft metal.

Chocks are wedged into the rock. They are not hammered. They do not damage the rocks. Today, nearly all climbers in North America use chocks. Climbers who use chocks are called clean climbers.

Clean climbers are conscious of the environment.

Helmets

A smart rock climber always wears a helmet. A helmet protects a climber's head. A helmet also protects the climber from falling rocks or other climbers who might fall from above. A helmet protects climbers if they fall a short distance before the belayer stops them.

Chapter 5

Today's Climbers

Recently, competitive rock climbing has become popular. Two or more climbers go up artificial walls as fast as they can. The winner is the climber who goes up the wall the fastest. These competitions attract thousands of fans.

Most climbers test only themselves, though. They stretch their physical skills. They enjoy being out among the beautiful scenery.

They work on their climbing skills. They try to climb difficult hills and mountains. Rock climbers' only competition is against themselves and nature.

Rock climbers are explorers. They explore their own abilities. They see how far their skills will take them. Many of them go places no person has ever been before.

Competitive rock climbs are races up a rock face.

Glossary

belayer—one who makes a rope secure

limber—when a person's limbs and joints are flexible; usually from exercise

outcropping—a piece of rock that sticks out from a rock face

rappel—to move down a cliff by sliding down a rope anchored at the top

rock face—the area of the hill or mountain that the climber goes up

sea level—standard for measuring height and depth using the level of the sea as zero

Sherpa—a group of people famous as mountain climbers living on the southern slopes of the Himalayas in Nepal

terrain—the specific features of a stretch of land

webbing—strong bands of fabric woven together

To Learn More

Hargrove, Jim and S.A. Johnson. *Mountain Climbing.* Minneapolis: Lerner Publications Company, 1983.

Hyden, Tom. *Rock Climbing Is for Me.* Minneapolis: Lerner Publications Company, 1984.

Long, John. *How to Rock Climb!* Evergreen, Colorado: Chockstone Press, 1989.

Skinner, Todd and John McMullen. *Modern Rock Climbing.* Merrillville, Indiana: ICS Books, Inc., 1993.

Walker, Kevin. *Learn Rock Climbing in a Weekend.* New York: Alfred A. Knopf, 1992.

Useful Addresses

American Mountain Guides Association
P.O. Box 4473
Bellingham, WA 98227

Geological Survey of Canada
601 Booth Street
Ottawa, ON K1A 0E8
Canada

Outward Bound
384 Field Point Road
Greenwich, CT 06830

U.S. Geological Survey
Map Distribution Branch
Box 25286
Federal Center
Denver, CO 80225

Internet Sites

Erik's Climbing Page
http://qlink.queensu.ca/~4eje/index.htm

Go Climb a Rock!
http://ic.net/~pokloehn

RockList
http://www.cmc.org/cmc/rocklist.html

The Adventures of Rock Jock
http://www.ldl.net/~skyler/alaska/index2.html

Index